Sonic Boom, Light Speed and other Aerodynamics What Do they Mean? Science for Kids

Children's Aeronautics & Space Book

BABY PROFESSOR

EDUCATION KIDS

Do you want to be a pilot?

Here are some terms for basic aeronautics you should know.

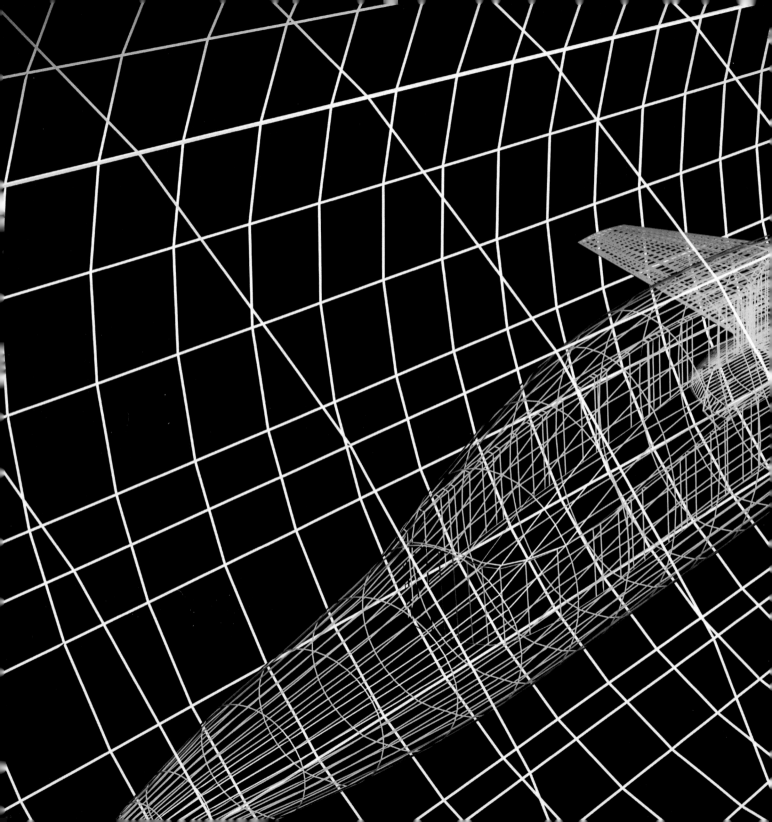

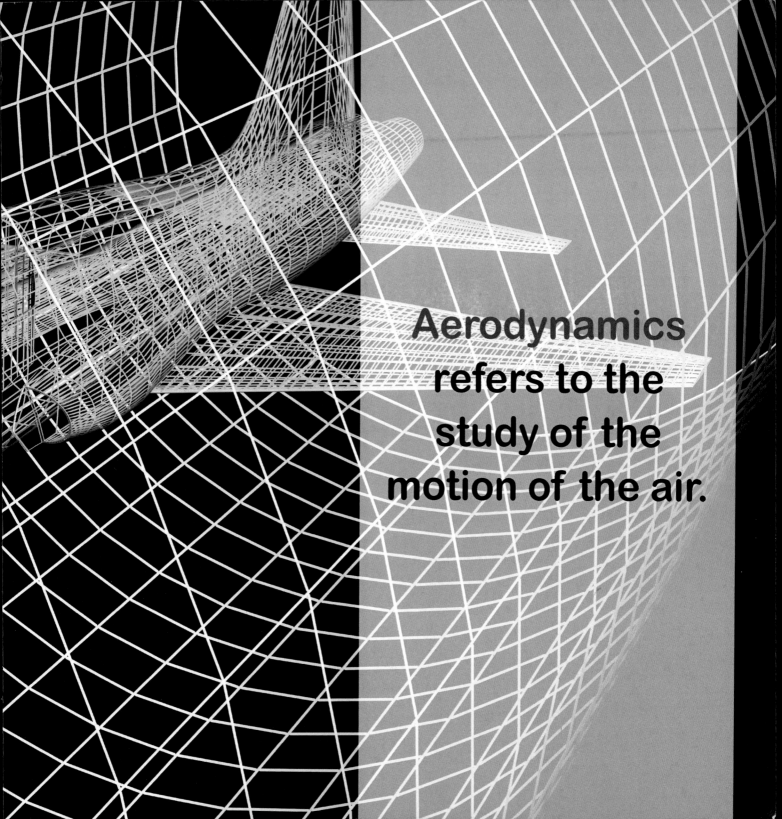

Aerodynamics refers to the study of the motion of the air.

Ailerons refers to the control surface found on the trailing edge of an aircraft's wings.

Aircraft is
a vehicle
that travels
through air.

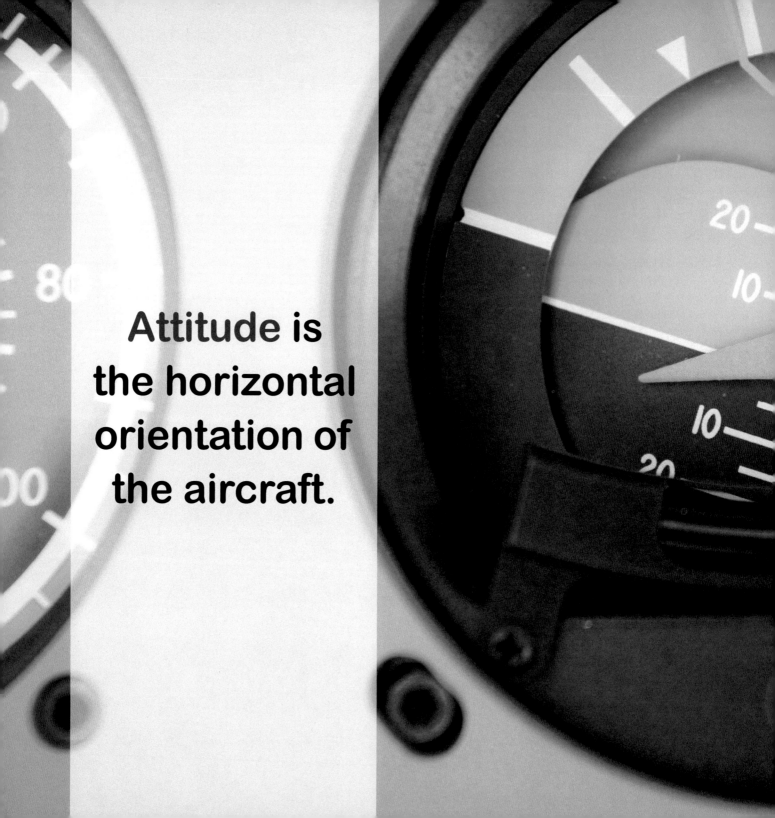

Attitude is the horizontal orientation of the aircraft.

Autogyro is an aircraft with unpowered wings and engine-powered propeller.

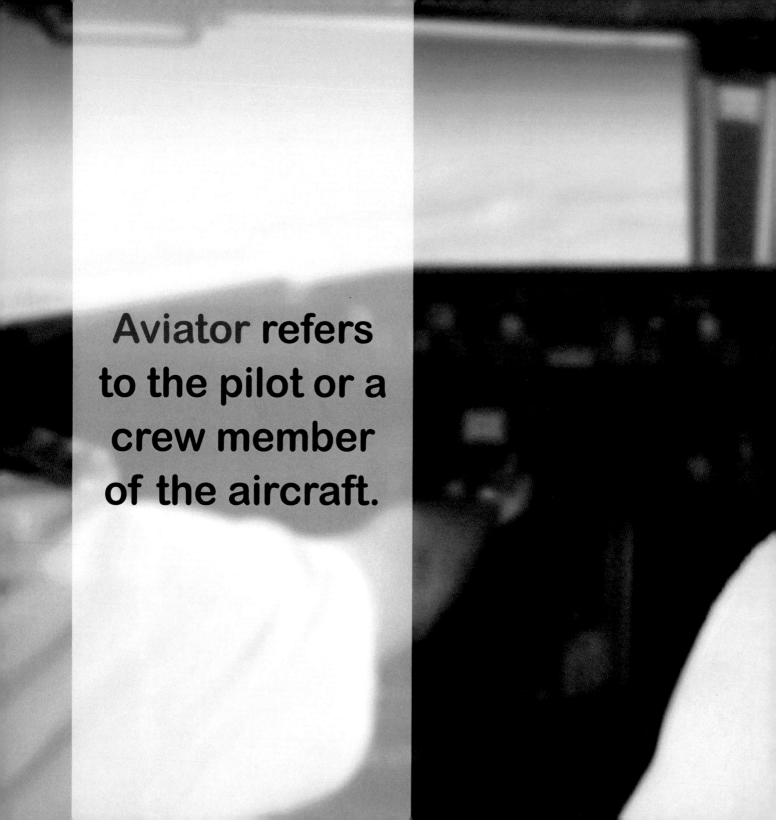

Aviator refers to the pilot or a crew member of the aircraft.

Flight level is the height of an aircraft above sea level.

Landing gear
is the structure
that supports
the aircraft when
not in the air.

Light speed refers to the speed of light while traveling in vacuum.

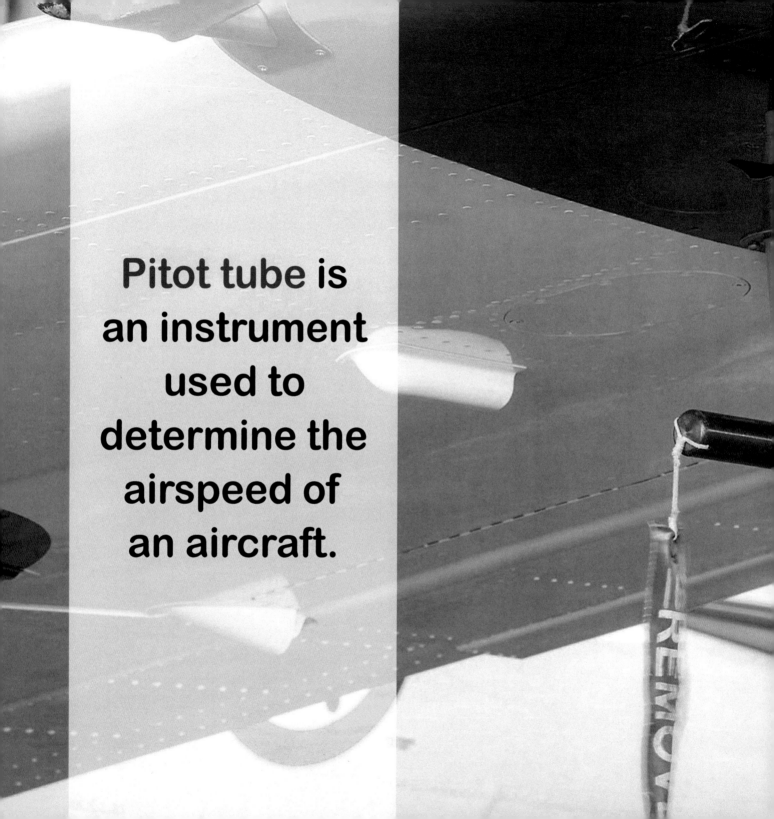

Pitot tube is an instrument used to determine the airspeed of an aircraft.

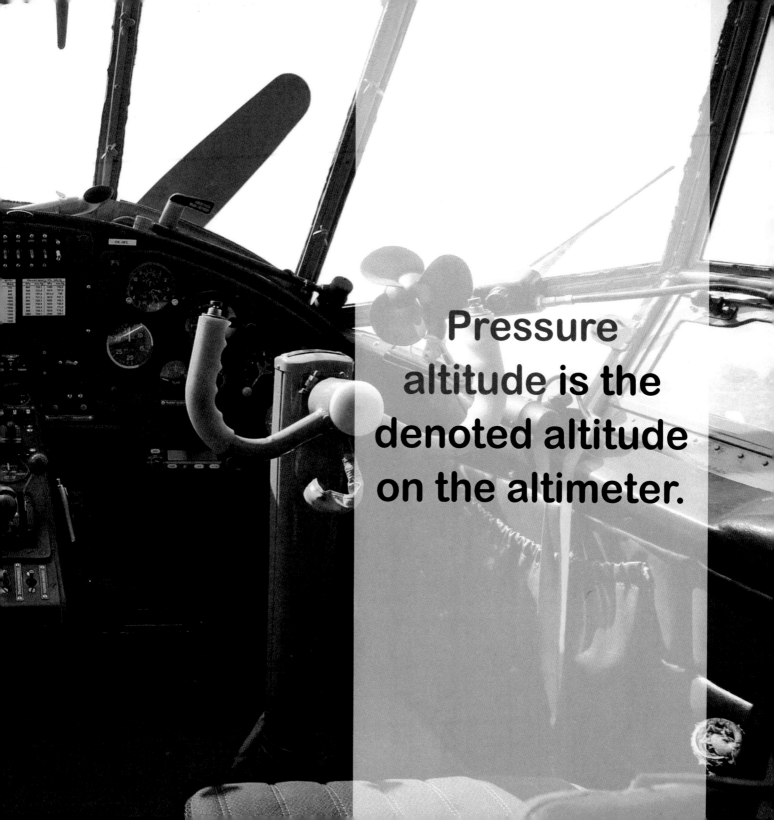

Pressure altitude is the denoted altitude on the altimeter.

Sonic boom
is the sound
created when an
aircraft passes
a series of
pressure waves.

Tailplane is the horizontal tail of an aircraft which includes the stabilizer and elevator.

Threshold refers to the starting part of the runway used for landing.

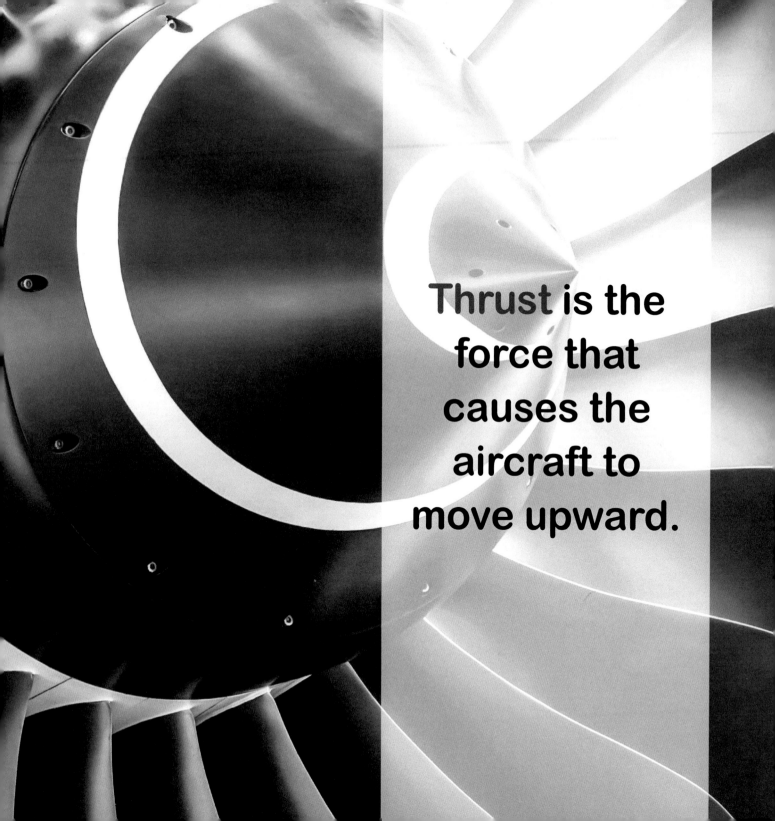

Thrust is the force that causes the aircraft to move upward.

Turbulence refers to the sudden and violent movements of air.

Wind shear refers to the sudden change of wind direction or speed.

There are more
aeronautic
terms,
research
and learn.
Have fun!

Visit

BABY PROFESSOR
EDUCATION KIDS

www.BabyProfessorBooks.com

to download Free Baby Professor eBooks
and view our catalog of new and exciting
Children's Books

Made in the USA
Las Vegas, NV
17 June 2021